INDIAN LIFE AND INDIAN LORE

IN THE LAND OF THE
HEAD-HUNTERS

The Eclipse Dance

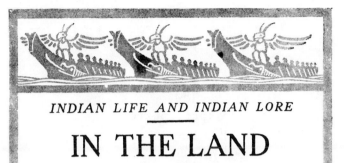

INDIAN LIFE AND INDIAN LORE

IN THE LAND
OF THE
HEAD-HUNTERS

By Edward S. Curtis
Author of "The North American Indian"

**ILLUSTRATED WITH PHOTOGRAPHS
BY THE AUTHOR**

A DOUBLE ELEPHANT BOOK

Ten Speed Press
Berkeley, California

First published in 1915 by the World Book Company.
For further information, write to:

1🖘

TEN SPEED PRESS
P. O. Box 7123
Berkeley, California 94707

Cover design by Nancy Austin
Book production by Hal Hershey

Library of Congress Catalog Card Number: 91-050672
ISBN 0-89815-421-9

First Ten Speed Press printing, 1974
Printed in the United States of America

1 2 3 4 5 — 95 94 93 92 91

FOREWORD

THIS book had its inception in an outline or scenario for a motion picture drama dealing with the hardy Indians inhabiting northern British Columbia. I submitted the scenario to my friend Robert Stuart Pigott, who urged that it be put into book form and that the declamatory style of the tribal bards be followed. Pigott is responsible for the suggestion; I am guilty of its execution; and we mutually have a deep affection for the little book. It is the outcome of one of those rare friendships which tend to make life worth living.

In the working out of the photo drama and the book, there came to be slight differences between the two; but in the main they are the same, and both give a glimpse of the primitive Americans as they lived in the Stone Age and as they were still living when the hardy explorers Perez, Heceta, Quadra, Cook, Meares, and Vancouver touched the shores of the Pacific between 1774 and 1791.

Astonishment has been expressed that headhunting existed among the North American Indians, notwithstanding the fact that every explorer of the North Coast region mentioned this custom. The taking of heads was a common

practice along the Pacific Coast from the Columbia River to the Arctic. Much material bearing
upon this subject will be found in Volumes IX
and X of *The North American Indian*.

The Author

CONTENTS

IN THE LAND OF THE HEAD-HUNTERS

A somber, gloomy forest meets a forbidding sea

IN THE LAND OF THE HEAD-HUNTERS

PROLOGUE

FROM the wind-swept Straits of Fuca far to the North, a somber, gloomy forest meets a forbidding sea. Gnarled, twisted, and low-bent are the fir, cedar, and spruce which first breast the angry ocean winds, and worn the cliffs which throw back the ever-beating, roaring surf. Countless small islands stand sentinel-like off those shores, forever meeting the dashing waves which cast their spray across them. Near and far, snow-capped peaks thrust their rugged, cloud-wrapt forms from the forest green to the sky. Here and there gulfs and straits break through this outer bulwark of rock and forest. From these spring innumerable waterways,—bays, fiords, and sounds,—reaching north, east, south, and west, through some of which the flooding, ebbing tide sweeps with sullen, devouring roar. Almost everywhere on these inland waterways the mountain forest reaches the water's edge, and at flood tide the branches touch the water.

The winters are long, gloomy seasons of wild, lashing winds and ceaseless rains.

1

Snow comes for but a short time to give this land a coat of white. The months of May, June, July, and August are summer, and afford days of such delight, with forest and snow-peak mirrored in the calm sea, that one is prone to believe the summer is for always, and that such scenes of quiet beauty cannot so soon change to violent storm.

The forests and mountains possess their share of wild life. In the high mountain meadows graze the elk, and in mountain meadow, in forest marsh, and by the sea's edge are the feeding deer. Among the serrated crags of the snow-covered peaks the mountain goats feed in numbers scarcely found elsewhere. On the mainland the great brown bear wanders, leaving tracks so large that one can scarcely believe one's eyes. On the islands, as well as on the mainland, the black bear is everywhere about, and through the forest, by land and stream, along the endless shores of the inner seas, play, hunt, and prowl the cougar, wolf, lynx, marten, mink, otter, beaver, and raccoon. In the air, from sea to mountain-peak the great bald eagle soars in watch for prey. Of song birds there are few. It is as if these forests were too vast and gloomy for their liking. The crow, the raven, the hawk,

The sea itself teems with life

the owl are everywhere about. Of water
birds there is no end. Geese, swan, and
brant are seen largely on their north-
ward and southward migrations. For the
smaller birds the rocky islands are nesting
places, and there the birds in flight are
like clouds. The sea itself fairly teems
with life: whale, sea-lion, seal, porpoise,
halibut, salmon, cod, herring. The sands
and rocks abound with shell-fish. The sea
bed is so covered with plants and sea
anemones, that to look into the crystal
depths is to glance into fairyland.

The native dwellers in this land are sea-
going people whose character seems in
harmony with their gloomy, forbidding
homeland. In warfare they are head-
hunters with small regard for life, and
ceremonial cannibalism is not unknown.
Their mentality is to the Caucasian diffi-
cult of comprehension, and their conclu-
sions are seemingly inverse. Pride of
caste, position,—"highness," as they term
it,—is the foremost tribal thought, and the
ways of maintaining, increasing, or losing
such highness form the story of their lives.
Success or failure in every effort is depen-
dent on the spirits, good or evil. It matters not whether it be the taking of small
fish, the capture of the largest whale, or
success in war,—spirits govern all.

During the summer months these people attend well to the gathering of food, largely from the sea, going from place to place where food is abundant. During the winter months of dark rain and wind they gather in their fixed villages, where occur the winter ceremonies or dances. These great ceremonies are quite different from any seen among other Indians of North America. They afford the entertainment which helps to pass the long winter months, and serve to increase the position of the giver. Striking and often fearful are the scenes of these winter revels.

Such was the country, thus lived the people, when the white man first touched these shores.

To rocky, surf-beat islets my canoe has borne me

CHAPTER ONE

THE VIGIL

"Some strange evil, like an angry, winged monster, hangs above me! I feel the gloomy clouds gather close about me, and a hand like icy Death grips my heart. I drive my canoe through the boiling surf, and the voice of the angry ocean mocks me.

"For half one moon's life I have fasted—I have wandered. To rocky, surf-beat islets my canoe has borne me. To dizzy peaks of farthest mountains I have climbed. Four times each day have I bathed my body. The cougar and the bear have I met and with them counseled. By my grandfather's grave, with skulls and bones about me, I have watched the stars and prayed. I have prayed to the Spirits of the Ocean; to the Spirits of the Mountain; to the Spirits of the Wind; I have prayed to the Spirits of the Dead: still my heart has had no answer. Yet, worse than that, tomorrow woe comes upon the land.

"Halfway on his journey the Sun will meet an all-devouring monster. Midday will be like night. With scream and croak the eagle and the raven will find perches in the gloomy forest. The owl, companion of evil and darkness, will sweep the air with hoot and jeer.

"Every law but one have I followed in my vigil, and now in the final plea I will build the sacred fire. Through the day and through the

9

darkness I will keep it burning and to the spirits make my invocation. Then will my fasting cease, and to my mind will come the thought of food and earthly life.

"Flame and Smoke! Flame and Smoke! Climb
    ye higher! Reach and hold the angry mon-
    ster who would our Sun devour!
Spirit creatures of the East Wind!
Spirit creatures of the West Wind!
Spirits of the South and of the North!
Come close and give me strength.
Spirits of the Ocean! of the Earth! of the Sky!
Bring me strength! Through long fasting my
    legs are weak.

"Strange sounds are in my ears. The stars dance madly! What weird figures weave themselves in the curling flames? What vague faces in the waving smoke? The smile of a maiden? Has my mind wandered for an instant from the vigil? I hear the far-off voices of the ocean. 'Tis like the maiden's chant. Ah! My eyes are heavy. They close in sleep.

"The night is past. The fire is dead, my vigil ended. Have peace and strength reached my heart? No! No! The spirits did not come, for in that final hour my mind broke the foremost law. I thought of a maid, and in the flame and smoke I saw her face!

I have prayed to the Spirits of the Wind

"Once more I must fast and languish ere peace can fill my heart.

"Listen!

"Is my brain still in trance? Truly no, for on the crest comes swiftly a canoe of cedar. Stately sits Naida, the proud chief's daughter. Closer now, and now passing, is the canoe of the chieftain's daughter. To my ear is borne her song of pride, of love and longing. It is the daughter of the great War Chief Waket, and hers was the face in the waving smoke!

"That picture was a dream, and ever do dreams our footsteps lead. My father knows no victor! His son can let his heart go where it will! With rapid stroke of paddle I will overtake the maid, the War Chief's daughter, and with songs of love and wealth will woo her."

CHAPTER TWO

MOTANA MEETS THE PRINCESS

"Proud Prince, pursue me not with words of your father's wealth. Sing not to me songs of love and longing. It is not seemly that prince and princess should woo like beasts or slaves! Let Kenada send his clansmen bearing gifts with song and declaration. It is in council long and serious that the Princess' hand is pledged."

"Your words of law and logic are very true, but in my fasting, in my hours with the spirits, our souls have met. When laws of Earth and Spirits meet in conflict, Earth rules must surrender in defeat. Let us sit by the brook and watch the rushing water. Perhaps its words will give us wisdom.

"You say that skulking in the shadows you saw the face of the Sorcerer Chief? Do not tell me that grizzled monster wants you for his wife! Truly it is not fit that gentle Spring and ugly Winter wed. The Sorcerer's songs are few and evil,—his deeds of valor less. How can the great War Chief of countless coppers [1] give heed to one so poor, so ugly, so old? It cannot be that his songs of dark and evil magic fill your father's heart with fear. You say for many moons this Sorcerer has in darkness chanted

---

[1] A "copper" is an oblong plaque made from native copper, decorated with heraldic design in low relief. Each plaque bears a name, and doubles in value with every change of owner until it reaches a value of many thousand dollars. Thus it is both a crest and visible evidence of wealth.

14

I will overtake the maid, and with words of love and wealth will woo her

prayers of evil incantations. Yes, I know it is common rumor that lives of men, like autumn leaves, fall before his incantations; but war clubs, spears, and slings can easily defeat his songs of evil magic.

"My people's village, Awati, is the largest of the nation. Four days more I will fast and pray; then homeward across the raging surf I will make my way. To my father I will bare my heart and plead to take for wife the daughter of Waket. And when the Awati clansmen go to beg for Waket's daughter, they will be spokesmen for my father and his many warriors. In smooth and oily words will our clansmen beg her hand; but should Waket, fearful of the Sorcerer's evil magic, refuse their presents and decline to give his daughter, the clansmen then will show their claws and say: 'We come not here with empty hands or with feeble words, for in the darkness of the night Kenada's war canoes have drawn close, and resting on the quiet waters just beyond the headland, are all the war canoes of his nation. Play not with words of fear or greed, but quickly tie your strength with Kenada, richest, bravest chief of all.'

"Well will your father know that to refuse the Raven Chief will mean war and slaughter.

"I look into your eyes. I touch your lips. Go now, Naida, to your father's home and say to him, 'I have dreamed of love. In eight sleeps will come a great chief to claim me for his son.'

"Go now, beloved!
O that I might go, beloved, to sit beside thee,
    love of mine!
O that we might go, beloved, walking hand in
    hand along the misty path of copper!"

Along the misty path of copper

CHAPTER THREE

MOTANA JOURNEYS TO THE ISLAND OF THE DEAD

"AGAIN I turn my thoughts from maids, from food, from worldly things, and think of songs and magic. To yonder gloomy Island of the Dead my canoe will take me. Through the tangled, gruesome jungle I will make my way. In tree above me, in cave beside me, in box, canoe and bundle, are the Dead!

"Once more I feel the weakness of my fasting, and the singing in my ear.

"This singing! Is it the voice of the Dead?

"My footsteps lead me on through ever-deepening gloom. Tonight I sleep upon the bed of Skulls.

"I start! I tremble! What was that?

"I hear the rattle in the tree-tops far above me! Do the Ghosts walk and mock me?

"With whir and thud a bleached and broken skeleton strikes the earth beside me.

"Ha! The Spirits try my courage by dropping bones upon me.

"Darkness gathers in the somber forest.

"On I hurry over rocks and through the tangle. A lakelet stands before me. On its placid surface I see the dancing new-born Moon.

"Now I bathe my body and with strokes slow and sure I cross the water, for on the other shore is the House of Skulls. Great is the magic of

that fearsome House of the Dead.   Rare is the
youth who braves a night of vigil there.   Its
floor is a solid pack of mouldering skulls; its
roof-supporting posts are festooned from ground
to eaves with scores of others; beneath its rafters
swing leering mummies and grinning heads!

"If all were brave enough to spend a night in
vigil here, small pride would the heart possess.
I put my foot upon a skull:—

"What matters it that you were once the
greatest chief of all?

"And you beneath my other foot:—

"Perhaps you were once a singer of songs? a
maker of magic? a talker with the Spirits?

"What is the answer now?

"If I sleep here, perhaps these Ghosts will
draw about and give the answer.

"Darkness, full and somber, creeps across the
land.   With the passing of the light is born the
ghostly spirit of the Night.

"The unseen ones of fiery eyes hurtle here and
there amid the ghostly shadows.

"The breeze-blown trees sway! whisper! almost groan!

"Bats squeak! Birds scream!

"The very air seems filled with ghostly things.

"Snakes and crawling lizards! Toads, omen of
death, hop from skull to skull, and blink their
sleepy eyes.

"He who from the House of Skulls would win
supernatural power must keep its laws. Stand-

I will bathe my body—I will cleanse it of the foulsome thing

ing here, well do I remember the words of the Ancient Faster: 'My son, when your footsteps take you there, be brave. Untie the mummy from its scaffold and place it well upon your back; fasten its bony arms well around your neck and let them grip fast; then plunge four times beneath the water. Now make your couch upon the skulls and close your eyes in thought or sleep.'

"Is my heart brave enough to spend the night's long hours with that most hideous thing clasped about my neck? Surely the son of the great chief whose totem is the Raven, does not fear darkness or the dead!

"I am faint. I am weak from days of fasting. Let me close my eyes and rest.

"What strange things see I in my fearful night of dreams?

"Weird creatures dance before my eyes. Birds, beasts and supernatural monsters of the deep rush at me. A hundred skeletons take flesh and clamor for my life!

"Ah!

"The fearful, gruesome night is past. I will bathe my body. I will cleanse it of the foulsome thing.

"Then with the sun I journey, and far upon the distant highest peak of Stony Mountain I will build my sacred fire."

CHAPTER FOUR

THE VISION

"Long does my sturdy craft breast wave and tide. On Stony Island's snow-white, shell-strewn beach I land. Through the jungle, through the swamp, I take my way to the very topmost peak. Now, I build again the sacred fire. Four times each day ten songs I sing, and every song will be for supernatural power.

"That his first son might be a hunter and a warrior was my father's constant prayer. While I was yet in my mother's arms, he with his spear in deadly struggle met the grizzly bear. With pride he brought me to the monarch slain and placed my hands upon his paws, and cried, 'Ho, strong one of the forest! Now you are dead we beg your power, we beg the great strength of your claws. Ho, slain one! This my son will eat the fragments of your heart that he may have endurance and ferocity.'

"Then, that I might know stealth in war, a wolf was brought, and placing my hands upon its forefeet, he, my father, prayed, 'O sly one of the wilderness! We come to beg the slyness of your paws. We eat your heart for stealth and courage.'

"Then prayers and songs were offered to the squirrel, that fleetness likewise to my feet might come. And last of all, the eagle was begged for power to see afar and strike with quickness.

Long does my sturdy craft breast wave and tide

"I sing my songs and pray far into the starry night, while through my memory all these teachings flow. Song and words leap back from glen to peak, and then the Echo Spirits hover everywhere about.

"I sing:

"O Echo Ones! Protect and guard me!
Bring your baskets filled with plenty, filled with
good health and cheer.

"A strange note in the Echo call comes from afar. It is a song of love. The Echoes sing of smiles, of laughter and content, but not of earthly love. The voice draws nearer.

"It is not a spirit, black or fair, but a maid to tempt me from my vigil.

"Begone, you with your caressing words! Do you not know the law—that in the vigil one may give no thought to women?"

"Do not spurn me. You believe in dreams and visions. While sleeping in my father's house, I dreamed that the proud son of Kenada returned my love. I saw our hearts bound in the sacred hoop of cedar."

"Away, shameful thing! Your thoughts, your words, are born of evil not in maiden's dreams. With every word I see a serpent in the flame."

"You dare to spurn my love, and I the daughter of the great Sorcerer? Short life to you, O foolish youth!"

"Away, you bold and evil one!   These are my days of songs and prayers.

"With this long fasting, how clear has grown my brain!   I walk with the lightness of a feather. My body almost floats upon the air.   The drifting clouds grow rosy with color of dawn, golden with the tints of dying day.   The breeze from mountain dale fans my brow with perfume of springtime.   The whispering pines and droning bees now lull my brain to rest.

"Long have I slept.
"What strange and fanciful dreams!
"How great the journey of my shadow!
"I sat alone beside my fire.   I wept, for I was far away in No Man's Land.   Again I wept. An evil something crept upon me.   I tried to move, but could not.   The touch of a hand was on my face.   Then the serpent creature crept away, and all was peace.   I heard a mighty whistling through the air.   Filled with terror, I could scarcely lift my eyes.   Before me stood a great white bird, gazing at me.   The spell of its eye held me, controlling thought and action.   I laid myself upon its back, my arms around its neck.   The mighty bird rushed forward on the ground, then rose slowly, heavily, higher and higher, in a great ascending spiral, through clouds, through mists, with onward rush till all

Motana, son of the Raven Chief

the earth was lost to view. At last it perched upon the topmost crag of a strange and ghostly world. There was no sun, there was no moon, there was neither heat nor cold. Day was night and night was day.

"The monster bird took flight, circled and circled until it passed from sight. Alone, I looked about and wept. While yet I wept, I heard again the whistling roar of its flight. With a rush of air it came to rest. Again I climbed upon its back, and in a great encircling glide it soared and soared through mist and cloud.

"At last it left me on the lower plains of the uncanny Shadow World. Here was a stream, beautiful, murmuring, soothing, lulling. Its course lay straight before me. Entwining, ghostly trees arched its way, swaying, drooping heavy with owls, the Spirits of the Dead.

"Away with this hour of dreams!

"What strange thoughts oppress me?

"The spirits have been close, and supernatural power is mine, I know. My heart should sing with joy.

"Yet some vague voice warns me of disaster— I touch my throat!

"Ha!

"My necklace stolen!

"Locks of my hair have been cut!

"It was that spurned messenger of the black and evil Sorcerer who has stolen my hair, my necklace of teeth and claws. No doubt the very

breath of my body has been taken.   Even now
they are chanting their songs of short life for me.
Could I but close my eyes and see as Spirits see!

"There in a somber glade three men sit by a
smouldering fire, their faces black.   Their words
are low and hushed.   Their leader is the Sorcerer who would wed my sweetheart.   To win
her hand he would take my life with evil magic.

"Now comes that vicious maid whom late I
spurned, and in her hands are my hair, my necklace!

"Yes, and in a ball of springy softness, my
very breath!

"The Sorcerer smiles his glee, murmuring,
'Well done, my daughter.   Bring the grave box,
bring the toads.'   Chants the one of evil magic,
'Within these withering toads we place his life,
and as they wither and decay, so shall he!'

"Before my flesh can wither through their evil
incantations, Awati's war canoes shall sweep
upon the village and quickly prove the real
'short-life bringer' to be club and spear.

"My vigil now is ended.   Westward I will
take my way to my father's village.   Above me
spreads a dome of gold, flecked with feathery
tufts of drifting crimson.   Before me lies a
dancing path of gold and copper.

"There where the sky and dancing trail meet,
sinks the wondrous globe of fire.

"O Thou, the great Life-Giver!

"Grant me strength for all Life's trails.

Naida, the proud princess

"One by one the stars come blinking out, and there above me stretches the flickering Milky Way from sea to sea. The sea itself is molten stars, through which ten thousand denizens of the deep rush onward, leaving their trails of liquid fire. Close by, with spout and plunge, sports the great blue whale. Seals lift their glistening, dog-like heads from the phosphorescent sea. A school of porpoise, like wheels of gleaming silver, flash before me."

CHAPTER FIVE

MOTANA'S RETURN

At the gray coming of day Motana reached his father's village, and great was his welcome there. So long had he wandered, his mother had dreamed of disaster and wept with fear. Straightway he begged his father to call in council all the head men, that they might hear the story of his vigil.

"My father will tell you that, as is the way of the Kwakiutl, he sent me on this journey, to fast, to pray, to talk with the Spirit Ones of the Earth, of the Sky, of the Air and the world of the Dead. All these laws have I followed, and have found much knowledge.

"Now, as it is with men, I have met a maid. Her words are soft, her eyes are deep. She is the daughter of the Chief Waket. The Sorcerer, whose evil magic is known throughout the land, would wed her. Even now he is singing songs to take my life. Will my father's warriors go tonight to demand this princess for my wife?"

Loud rose the voice of Kenada, urging his warriors to prepare for battle. "We will go with presents and with honeyed words, our claws concealing. Should Waket and his people hesitate in answer, our battle cry will chill their blood."

"Away! Away for preparation!" they shout.

Will my father's warriors go tonight to demand this princess
for my wife?

"Let us demand Naida and crush the Sorcerer, who would dare to sing songs of death to Motana!"

In the twilight, through the night, in the half-light, half a hundred great war canoes sped across the water. At the coming of the dawn, without a sound, without a call, they drew close within the shadows of a landlocked bay. With the gathering darkness on they sped again, every word a whisper, every needed signal the call of a bird of air or water. With the fading of the stars the fleet drew near the village of Waket. Again without call or sound they slipped within the shadow of the shore.

Two canoes sped toward the village. Eight slaves each drove them on. Standing in the bows, dressed in all their finery, were the messengers to beg the hand of Waket's daughter. Quickly they neared the village of the princess and with voice carrying loud and far they cried: "Ho, Waket, the greatest chief of all! We come like humble slaves as spokesmen for the mighty Chief Kenada, who would beg that you give your proud daughter Naida to his son. Though we come as beggars, we come with wealth of presents."

Called back the spokesman for Waket: "Great are your master's words, great his war deeds, measureless we know his treasures of slaves, canoes, and blankets. Proud would Waket be to link his family with so great a chief; but Naida is already pledged to the Sorcerer of Yilis and presents given."

In answer cried Kenada's messengers: "Ho, Waket! Give back the presents. Take back your words. Kenada is the richest chief of all. His rivals are buried deep beneath his wealth. Fear not the wrath of the aged Sorcerer! Grim death is close upon him. He is making black and evil magic to destroy our proud Motana. His short-life songs are like double-headed serpents, and will strike back upon their maker. All too long has this evil singer lived. Before another sun he will forever cease to sing."

"Ho!" cried the spokesman of Waket, "your words are big, but let us see your deeds. When the canoe of Kenada bears upon its prow the head of the Sorcerer, he may claim our princess."

"Ho! Your word is given. When tomorrow's sun is half upon its journey, our chief will claim your princess."

Messengers to beg the hand of Waket's daughter

CHAPTER SIX

THE DEATH OF THE SORCERER

Across the water, noiseless as a bird in flight, shot the canoes of Kenada to strike the Sorcerer's village in the dark and sleeping hours.

Now the fearful strife is on. Everywhere rings the cry:

"You sing short-life songs to Motana!"

Everywhere ring screams of rage and hate and fear.

Above the din and roar bellows the voice of Kenada:

"You dare sing short-life songs against the son of Kenada!

"He who plays with death must pay the price.

"Your last evil song is chanted.

"I take your head as marriage gift to the princess you would wed!"

Soon the bitter struggle ended.

With songs, with heads, with loot of slaves and goods, Kenada went again to the village of Waket, and when the sun was halfway on his journey, claimed the princess. Happy were the hearts of Motana and Naida.

Through the village ran the herald, calling, "Ho, ye! Ho, ye! The people of Waket and the people of Kenada are bound in friendship, for the hearts of the two great chiefs will be tied in marriage."

Loudly they called: "Waket bids the chiefs

and head men to gather in his great house for
feast and dances. Through all the night will we
feast, sing, and be merry. The dancers of every
clan and crest will don their masks and costumes.
The Raven and the Bear will show the dances
they were taught, and the Wolf will howl and
leap."

With the coming of the morning, Kenada and
his warriors took their homeward way.

When close upon his village, Kenada, stand-
ing upright in his great canoe, cried out: "Ho,
my people! This is a great day for our village.
On our quest we have won Waket's daughter.
In strife of battle we have met the people of the
Sorcerer's village and have taken many heads.
While we laugh and sing in victory, our hearts
are filled with tears. Our brave warriors Walas,
Yumkas, and Halam lost their lives in battle.
Mothers, wives, sweethearts, children, wail not,
weep not. Let others mourn and cry for you.
For every life we lost, we took ten. With ten to
do your weeping, truly your tears should turn to
smiles."

With shrieks and wails, wives and lovers
proved that the wailing of a thousand enemies
could not bring back the loved ones.

"Head men, warriors, hunters, clansmen
young and old! In the moon of spawning
salmon we will take the daughter of Waket for

Motana and his father, Kenada the Raven Chief

my son's wife.   The son of a chief so great must
have a new-made home of size beyond compari-
son.   Let every man who calls me chief put
forth his hand.   Some with maul and chisel will
fell great cedars.   Others with heavy maul and
wedge will split the planks.   Those with skill
and cunning will prepare four great posts of
cedar and carve upon them the whale, the bear,
the wolf, the eagle, and the raven.   Lagos, the
most skillful carver of all, will cut and fashion the
great post that stands before the house, as guar-
dian of the home.   On it he will carve all my
crest,—creatures of the ocean, creatures of the
land, and creatures of the sky.   When posts,
beams, and planks are ready, I will call together
all our people and quickly build the house.''

CHAPTER SEVEN

THE MARRIAGE OF MOTANA

FROM the village of the princess, Waket's heralds went from north to south, and with voices loud and strong announced the wedding of Naida and Motana. Called they: "Ho, ye! Ho, ye! Four moons ago the canoes of Kenada came to beg the daughter of our proud chief. Great is the chief who thus came begging for our richest gift, and vast the wealth of presents he brought to prove his pride and tribal standing. Long the lines of slaves who bore the gifts of furs, shells, blankets, robes, and masks. Canoes and coppers further formed the marriage gift. Proud should our daughter be. In the history of our village no other maid has been pledged with gifts so rich. Through many days have we made and gathered gifts, that our princess may not hang her head in shame when tomorrow the proud Motana comes to claim her.

"Ho, ye! Ho, ye! Wives of every house, prepare much food, for great must be the wedding feast."

Scarce had the sun started on its daily journey before all the village was astir with anticipation of the wedding. From house to house hurried women, old and young, slaves and nobles. On a throne of graven figures sat the chief's daughter, dressed all in furs, bedecked in trinkets carved from shell and metal. She sat demure, as

Soon we shall hear their songs of pride and boasting

a maiden should, with downcast eyes, awaiting
the wedding hour.   Everywhere upon the look-
out stages perched watchers scanning the distant
sea.   Then the cry rang out:

"They come!   They come!"

And the heralds cried:

"Their canoes are so many, they are like a
flight of birds skimming the water.   Closer yet
they come.   Soon we shall hear their songs of
pride and boasting.   They will try to make us
small with songs of crests, of coppers, with songs
of great eating, and their war deeds.

"Now we hear their singing, their shouting,
and the beating of the baton.   In the great war
canoe that leads the van stands the mighty Thunder Bird.   Now he flaps his wings and we hear
the thunder roar.   Right it is that the thunders
roar, for in the days of old that mighty roaring
Spirit of the Clouds brought us marriage laws.
One law it brought was that the man who would
take a maid for wife must show his courage, and
by strength of hand and arm prove the right to
take her.   He is landing now with his band of
sturdy warriors, and the young men of Waket
rush forward in mimic battle, that this proud
young man may find worthy foes who strike
blows thick and fast."

Short and sharp was the battle.   Bruised and
limping were those who met its brunt.   Thus did
the youth prove himself worthy of a wife.

The battle ended, the Thunder Bird flapped his

wings, the canoes rolled in the water, and again the thunders roared. The mystic bird of storm and thunder rushed upon the land. The grizzly bears, the wolves, the ravens, and the Tsonoqua with pomp and antic followed close behind. Then came all the people, weighted with presents. Long the boastful, stiff, and formal talk of giving. Then with pomp and splendor the bride was borne from her father's home to the canoe of her youthful husband. Stepping high, half flying, with pride the Thunder Bird perched upon the bow of the wedding barge, and then across the water with a roar of thunder and a song of victory the party took its way.

Waket, the great War Chief

CHAPTER EIGHT

YAKLUS AVENGES THE DEATH OF HIS BROTHER THE SORCERER

YAKLUS was a chief feared throughout the nation. In speech he roared and barked like an old bull sea-lion. In warfare he severed head from body with a single stroke. His warriors were but little less gorilla-like. His village stood on a rocky shore where the waters rushed, roared, and spumed. And with the ebb and flow of every tide sucking whirlpools, like ever-hungry maws of ocean monsters, waited for their prey.

For many days had this fearful chief made preparations for war. Extra bow-strings and arrows sharp had he counseled, also many spears, clubs, knives, and slings. Canoes were polished and armor made. Their foremost men of magic lived from the tribe apart, and with songs and incantation begged the spirit ones for visions of the journey.

The very day the village of Kenada was in marriage revel, Yaklus and his black-faced warriors sang their songs of farewell to home and family, then launched their canoes upon the rushing tide. If, on their way, they sighted luckless diggers of clams or takers of fish, they rushed upon them and destroyed them. Thus they went to the village of Kenada.

Little did Motana dream that on his wedding-day Yaklus was making ready for war upon his happy village. As he listened with delight to the rippling voice of Naida, he did not think that war and death were close upon him.

In the dark hours of sleep, death crept close to old and young, without a sound, without a cry of warning. So quick the muffled coming of the fleet, the dogs could scarce give warning before door, roof, and wall were rent asunder. Then came the fearful roaring war-cry:

"I am Yaklus, the short-life bringer! Prepare to die!"

All too well Motana knew the meaning of that dreaded cry. It was slaughter, pillage, and captivity.

Amid the din of yells, the thud of blows, the rending of planks, Motana clasped his bride and slipped through the secret door to the darkness of the forest. In whisper quick and low, "Be like a shadow while I rush to battle," he bade her. Scarcely had he spoken ere the crackle of burning wood and the roar of flames, mingled with crash of human conflict, almost drowned the fierce war-cry, the shriek of the wounded, the scream of the captives. As the lurid flames rose higher, they painted crimson the sea, lapping at the foot of a spectral forest.

In close and fearful conflict raged the battle where heads were pawns. Above all rose the cry:

"I am Yaklus, the short-life bringer!

As the lurid flames rose higher, they painted crimson the sea
lapping at the foot of a spectral forest

"Where is the great Raven Chief, and his proud son Motana?

"Let them come and try their strength!"

And again the cry:

"Spare no warriors or old women, but take for slaves young women and children!"

As only the doomed fight, fought Kenada. In the lurid glare the Yaklus horde thronged about him. Spears, clubs, and knives hurtled by his head. Men, like cougars, leaped upon him only to be thrown back as the elk tosses back the wolf.

Then the yelling mob with weight of numbers crushed him down.

Motana, young and supple, struck like an eagle here and there with fearful havoc to the foe.

Then a whizzing spear crashed through his body.

He tore the shaft away, reeling and staggering toward the heavy shadows. In the sickening, gripping agony of death he worked his way into the tangled blackness.

The fury of the battle was soon spent. The roar of flame and strife died low. Countless houses with great graven beams and posts were soon smouldering ruins, blackened snags.

Along the narrow beach where sea and forest meet, were strewn the headless ones. Few had escaped the vicious raid of Yaklus.

Yet some, beaver-like, had plunged into the water and slipped away with noiseless stroke, and others had groped and crawled into the dark, forbidding forest.

In the gray light of dawn, the gory Yaklus warriors turned away with shout and song.

What a fearful, ghastly sight the rising sun beheld!

There, on the beach, vulture, eagle, crow, and raven quarreled and fought.

Some mythic monsters on the seared and blackened posts laughed cruelly at man's pride of life: but others wept for sorrow. In the stillness, broken only by the quarreling of the birds, it was easy to imagine those carved, ugly creatures calling out:

"O foolish ones!
  But yesterday you sang your songs of life, of
      love:
  You boasted of your proud birthright and royal
      blood.
  Silent today, dead! Slave and noble are
      alike,—food for filthy birds!"

As the day wore on, there crept from the forest, singly or in pairs, the frightened few that had escaped. From a nearby island swam those who had braved the sea. Cut, bruised, and maimed were they.

From the jungle's shadows came a feeble, incoherent call. Some ran to see whence it came.

"It is Motana!"

In the gray light of dawn the Yaklus warriors turned away

"His body is rent and torn!"

"His soul has almost left it!"

"His spirit wanders now!"

Chego, the medicine healer, administered his potions, and sang his songs to recall the wandering mind. Before the day closed Motana's ravings ceased, his mind grew calm. With his first words he asked, "Where is Naida?"

Chego could only say, "Your heart must be brave, my son. In the flashing light she saw you fighting, saw you fall. Before she reached your side, the Yaklus warriors rushed upon her. Like the mother cougar she fought them back, but to no avail. They crushed her down and bore her away."

"Listen closely, you who speak with Spirits and sing songs of healing. To me have the Spirits also spoken. Had it not been so, I, like the others, would be dead upon the beach. Make me well, O Singer of Songs, that I may retake my Naida and destroy Yaklus the terrible one."

CHAPTER NINE

THE COMING OF THE WHITE MEN

"HI, yu, hi, yu,
Here and there, here and there,
This hand, that hand,
Right hand, left hand,
Left hand, right hand,
Which hand?"

With wild song and gesticulation, with bodies swaying and swinging in time with the singing and the drum of the baton, they played their game of chance. With steaming bodies, frothing mouths, heaving chests, they passed the pawn from hand to hand, while wilder grew the frenzy of the singing. Youths, maidens, and mothers loitered there to watch the game and listen to the gamblers singing.

A youth with terror in his face rushed in and fell among them. Gasping he cried out, "A monster bird flies low upon the water! Bigger than ten whales! It is near! It sweeps upon us!"

"To yonder headland, quick!" cried the leader. "Let the women and children flee to the forest."

Swiftly to the headland ran the warriors. Close grouped there, they watched the great thing sweep across the sea. What monster this, with great outstretched wings? Moving here and there were seen strange objects like parasites upon a whale.

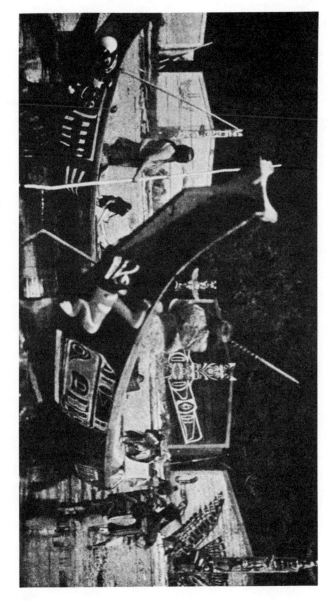

Strange sights met them at every turn

"Look! Look!" cried the keen-eyed one. "The crawling things are men. The monster bird must truly be a canoe of the spirit world, for men could not dream of one so great. It roars with thunder! Its mouth is belching smoke! Its wings are falling! Now it only drifts upon the water."

"Are the men upon its back flesh or spirits?" each asks the other.

"Yaklus, our great war leader, is away. We are too few to meet an enemy of a canoe so large. Perhaps our only safety is in flying to the forest, there to find the women."

"Chatter not of running like coward dogs, but watch close and count the men." Thus spoke the leader. "We have strong arms, we have slings, spears, bows, and knives. Why talk of leaving our houses, our crests, and all our goods for loot and fire? Let us prove our courage. Let us show Yaklus that he did not leave cowards to guard his village. Look again! A small canoe glides from the monster's back. They make the sign of presents. Truly we need not fear so small a party. Let us go with care to meet them. We will smile and answer them in signs of peace, but like a cougar watch their every action. If they prove an enemy, we will quickly take their heads."

With surprise and cunning the red men looked upon the white. They marveled, then questioned one another. Were the men of white skins and hair of every color, spirit creatures? Or were they men with red blood and white skins? With smiles and gestures the white men offered gifts in token of friendship and good will. And though the gifts were taken, the white men saw the looks of cunning and distrust. Their leader spoke:

"For safety's sake we had better awe them with our arms."

A gull sailed close above. Quickly a sailor raised a rifle, and with the roar and the smoke the gull dropped at their feet. A murmur ran through the group of red men. Whispered they:

"These may be men, but they kill by magic of thunder. Lest they take our lives, we will beg for friendship and try to learn or steal their magic."

With word and gesture the red leader quickly offered hospitality and promised gifts of skins and food. The red men led the way, the white men followed to the village.

Strange sights and smells met them at every turn. The odor of fish and blubber was everywhere. From pole to post leered and laughed the faces of the bear, the wolf, the whale, and mythic monsters. From the topmost point looked down the watchful eye of the eagle, the raven, and the bird of thunder. The portals of the great communal homes were devouring mouths of grotesque monsters.

Once within, the blood was almost chilled. Great, smoke-blackened, carved and figured posts and beams formed the frame. Planks

On the bow the mythic double-headed serpent rolled its eyes and darted forth its tongue

rived from great cedars formed the shell around
the somber, smoky, smelly gloom. The beaks,
wings, eyes, and jaws on the graven posts
flapped, rolled, and growled automaton-like.
Within them hollow, bellowing voices bade the
guests welcome. The guests felt as if they had
entered Hades and the Keeper of the Unfor-
tunates had in mockery called a welcome.

Scarcely had the explorers' eyes penetrated
the gloomy shadows when calls and shouts came
from every side. The tones rang tense and vi-
brant. The hardy explorers, although they did
not know the meaning of the alarm so quickly
given, felt their flesh creep, their blood tingle, as
they adjusted arms and ammunition. The leader of the red men saw their apprehension and
with reassuring gestures tried to make it known
that no harm was meant, that it was but the re-
turn of the great war chief from a foray.

CHAPTER TEN

THE RETURN OF YAKLUS

AROUND the wooded headland, where swaying boughs of fir and cedar swept the flood-tide's water, came the victory-reeking war fleet of the mighty Yaklus. The great canoe of this fierce warrior was in the lead. On its bow, as a decoration, the mythic double-headed serpent rolled its eyes and darted forth its tongue. Along the gunwales coiled the body of this writhing monster of the deep. On a high raised platform near the stern stood Yaklus; all about him lay gory heads, and at his feet huddled crouching slaves. Near the prow in costume partly human, partly animal, stood the soothsayer, the magician, forecaster of good and evil. Wild were the songs in which he led the victory-drunken warriors.

On to the village came the proud war fleet. Side by side in battle array the warriors stood. Then with a mighty shout they drove their great canoes upon the sand. The waiting ones on the shore rushed down to greet the victors. Everywhere was heard the shout and call:

"Husband!"

"Father!"

"Brother!"

"Are you safe?"

War is ever war, and lives must pay the price. Lifeless, mangled bodies of husbands, sons, and brothers are the pawns with which all battles are

Around the wooded headland came the victory-reeking war fleet

won or lost. When no answer came to a call, a
fearful, agonizing cry rent the air,—a howl,—a
wail,—the outburst of grief and anguish. Again
the incoherent, brutal shouting of the victors,
laughing, screaming to wives and mothers to
bring them cheer.

The warriors filed toward the village, on to
the great house of Yaklus the fearless. With
faces and bodies blackened proudly walked the
warriors. At their belts and trappings swung the
ghastly, gory heads of victims. Some dragged
captives doomed to slavery. Amid the hapless
ones walked the proud Naida. Little now to
show her pride of birth and station, and even less
to give her hope. Her captors fought like jungle beasts over so rich a prize, but quickly ended
this when Yaklus saw her beauty and heard her
name. "Let my slave keepers take her," he bel-
lowed, "and death to the one who molests her!"
Too well she knew her fate, knew there was no
hope of mercy from her father's bitterest enemy.

Now the heralds pass through the village
crying:

"Our great, our undefeated leader has returned, having overthrown the Raven Chief,
Kenada. Many heads and many slaves has he
brought. The village of the Raven Chief is
smouldering ashes. His head is here. His daughter, far-famed for beauty, is a slave in the great
chief's house. Yaklus bids us say this is a great
day for our nation. Never before has so strong

a war party gone forth. Never a battle so great have we ever won. And more, and more! Strange visitors have reached our shores this day. Their canoe is a mighty one with fearful wings. It speaks with thunder. The skin of these strangers is white, so white we think they must be gods! Yaklus bids all watch. If they are gods, we will learn their ways and get their wisdom. If they are but men and we like their way, we will make them welcome and bid them tarry. But if their ways are evil they will be as helpless as crippled crows. With a single song or call we can crush them. Tonight in the great house of Yaklus the head men will gather to give the Dance of Victory, and make welcome our strange guests. Great will be the dancing."

Banked thick against the walls was the motley throng of warriors and their wives

CHAPTER ELEVEN

THE DANCE OF VICTORY

WHEN full darkness fell on land and sea, began the revel. Glowing, snapping fires lighted the murky gloom. Flame and spark sprang upward through the smoke-hole of the roof. Banked thick against the walls was the motley throng of warriors and their wives. Food was brought in huge troughs and boxes. Proud chiefs vied with one another in gorging the rancid, oily stuff. Loud the boasting, the shouting, as they gulped the oil of fish, the blubber of whale, porpoise, and seal. Proud the man who could outdo the others.

While they feasted, laughed, and joked, the herald called the dancers, called with a voice loud and gruff:

"Yaklus, our chief, greatest chief of all, has won the greatest battle of our nation. Let us dance as we have never danced before. Let our maids show their grace of movement as they swing and glide in the flashing light. Let the fiendish grizzly bear with lolling tongue and red grimace show his ugly, awkward step. Let the tricky black bear do his dance with a swing and a whirl. Then the wasp with buzzing whir will chase them all away.

"Through the secret door will spring the terror-bringing Wild Man of the Woods. Though half man in form, he is thought to be all man in mind. Maybe his companions are of the evil spirit world. His bed is in a cave with wolf and bear. His dance is the most fearful of all, taught him by all the supernatural ones of forest and mountain. With wild gesticulations he will run, fly, growl, he will be bear, wolf, eagle, raven, porpoise, fish, and whale in turn. More than all this, he will imitate the supernatural ones.

"With all the Wild Man's knowledge of the forest, the ocean, the mountains, the spirit world, there is one mightier than he. It is the great and fearful Thunder Bird, the spirit of all those forces that we cannot see. With mighty roar and rumble he will sweep upon us from the somber clouds. He will not come until all the earthly ones have done their parts.

"The great bull elk with spreading antlers strides in, and all the women's hearts go a-flutter, for this proud one is great in love. Rare the maid who can resist his call. Fine will be the dance of this all-haughty one.

"But soon his dance will cease, and quick will be his flight when in leaps the grim Hamatsa, reminding us that life is only death. Today we make love in the springtime of life, tomorrow we are naught but skulls of death. Bleached skulls of man and maid dangle about the neck of this death reveler. But death is not all rattling skulls, for next we see the hypnotic dancing birds of the spirit world."

The dancing began. The beasts of the forest, the birds of the sky, the fish and monsters of the

Let the tricky black bear do his dance

deep, the spirit ones of earth and zenith, love and death, all with the blood-drunk warriors joined in that fearful revel. With rolling eye, with clacking, clanking beak and jaw, with growl, bark, croak, squawk, scream, and howl, whirled the dancers, while above their din rang the exultant cry of the warriors.

Then, led by the bereaved ones, those within and those without the great house began the fearful, blood-chilling howl for the dead. They clamored for revenge. They clamored for the life of Naida, daughter of the Raven Chief.

The howling, wailing shout went up:

"Our husbands!

"Our fathers!

"Our brothers!

"Are dead in the land of the Raven Chief!

"We want his daughter's blood!

"Yaklus has promised the greatest feast of all,—let us have the greatest feast of all!"

Up stood the mighty Yaklus; loud roared his voice:

"I am the greatest chief of all!"

In each hand he held four gory heads. With outstretched arms he shook them, crying:

"These prove the kind of man I am.

"Slaves and common people! would you dare to claim my hard-won captive?"

Wailed the surging mob:

"Life for life!"

Loud rang the voice of the chief:

"Women of my household! take the captive, bathe her, dress her, oil her hair, make her beautiful for life or death. Then we shall have the answer She shall dance with all her grace. She shall dance to show the charm of beauty. She shall dance the Dance of Life or Death! Does she please us, we will spare her. If not, we will throw her to the hungry wolves."

The wasp with buzzing whir will chase them all away

CHAPTER TWELVE

NAIDA DANCES THE DANCE OF LIFE OR DEATH

Too well Naida knew the slender thread that held her life. By supple swaying of her body she must fascinate the one she loathed and hated: he who had taken her father's life; he who had torn her sweetheart husband from her side. The women, mad with jealous hate, sneered and mocked while they made her ready.

"Proud princess, you think you are!"

"A beaten slave, at best."

"For you small chance of life."

"We will lead the mob when it clamors for your blood."

"You will dance, you will smile, but in vain!"

"Your head will pay for the lives your father took!"

Though she knew her hopeless situation, yet life is dear to all, even if gained by charming one so loathed and hated. Great her native beauty as she came within the fire's glow.

Wild her dancing, wild the singing as she danced.

With outstretched arms, with heaving chest and smiling lips, swaying, swinging she came quite close to the fearful chief.

Then with ever-present smile she retreated far within the shadows.

Quickly whirling, yet always smiling, she circled once more about the fire. When she came before the chief again, she put forth all her charm.

She smiled, she stretched her arms toward him.

With a shout he called:

"She dances well! Her life is spared. Let no man or woman dare molest her!"

Low, sullen growls were heard from those who thirsted for her life.

Jealous, bitter thoughts consumed the women of Yaklus' household.

Fiercer, wilder, more bestial grew the dancing. Louder the shouting of men and women. Fearful was the screaming of those who danced as bird or beast.

In the midst of all this revel, the mighty Bird of Thunder swooped upon them. With his coming rolled the mimic thunder. All the dancers bowed before him—he, the fiercest of the Spirit World. Before him, even the eagle and the grizzly bear gave way. When all were gone, the sacred bird with outstretched wings ran dancing forward and swept away into the darkness of the sky.

Filled with awe and wonder the white men rowed to their sturdy ship. Truly these were strange people they had met.

Naida dances the Dance of Life and Death

CHAPTER THIRTEEN

THE DEPARTURE OF THE WHITE MEN

THE next day brought many visitors to the white men's ship, to see what manner of canoe was theirs. The captain, his mind filled with pictures of severed heads, was fearful of attack.

It was scarcely midday when Yaklus, in stately pomp, embarked to call upon the ship. Twenty paddlers manned the high-bowed craft and swept it on with rhythmic shout and song. Their paddles cut the bright water. Four times the chief's canoe completely circled the white man's ship. Each encircling sweep brought the great chief nearer. Then with a shout the paddlers swing their great canoe close by.

A strange throng it was that climbed the rail. Rich and priceless gifts of furs it brought to show good will. By sign and gesture the men of Yaklus bade the white men welcome. Then they swarmed about the ship in wonder, till Yaklus called his men about him and asked the white men to visit his village, to see its ways and wonders. As he came, he went, with song and well-timed stroke of paddle. Four times his canoe swept round the ship. With each four strokes his men gave a shout and struck the gunwales with their paddles.

Scarcely had their visitors gone, before the explorers started toward the village. When they reached it they wandered here and there; beheld the carvers cutting strange, grotesque figures; saw the smelly food in preparation; watched the mothers following fashion's strange demands, flattening their babies' heads; saw the weavers making fabric; and received as presents every form of curious trinkets.

With the closing of the day the explorers returned to their good ship, glad to be safe upon her deck once more. For days they mended sails and spars, and traded for the fur of seal, otter, mink, and marten. With their repairs well done, their barters ended, they set sail for far-off lands. To see them sail away the warriors, young and old, launched their canoes, while the women stood chatting on the beach.

The warriors, young and old, launched their canoes

CHAPTER FOURTEEN

THE ESCAPE OF NAIDA'S SLAVE

So great was the excitement of the white men's going that for the time Naida was freed from prying eyes. She called a youthful fellow-captive, bade him follow closely her words.

"While all watch the departure of the white strangers, go quickly to the forest and hide. Wait until far into the night. Then creep out and in a small canoe start for our home. When daylight comes, hide again, and again with darkness speed away. Find our village, find the people. A voice tells me Motana is not dead. Find him! Give him this token. Tell him I await his coming. Tell him where I sleep. Tell him I will each night try to leave the secret door unfastened. Let him creep within and touch me, but speak not. I shall know his touch and we will fly away. Heed well my words. May your heart be brave, your arms strong. Now away, and hide with care, for if they find you we are lost!"

Quickly he sped to the forest and far within its shadows he climbed high in a thick branched tree. There he clung to trunk and limb, waiting for the passing of day. Searching parties scurried back and forth through the forest's tangle, looking beneath logs and in the fern-grown bramble, but not into the forest tops. Crouching above them, the boy heard their dire threats of beheading when they found him.

The night was full half spent before he ventured from his hiding. Crawling, creeping, listening, he found a canoe and sped away, away with all the strength of desperation. When dawn came, he dragged his frail craft into the tangle of the shore and crept far in to sleep through the day. Once he was awakened by his pursuers as they paddled close along the shore. When the voices died away, he slept again. At the close of day he awoke and watched the disappearing sun across the kaleidoscopic sea of blue, green, crimson, orange,—watched it sink to rest in billowy clouds of fire.

As the fires of the western sky died low the crimson grew somber in the darkness, and on the limpid surface the crescent moon danced like a feather of the swan. Then the fearless lad sped on again across the waters. The rush, the roar, the whirlpool of tidal rapids he met and mastered. On, on through the darkness he drove his craft toward the ancient Raven Village.

At break of day he crept into the forest and slept. One more night would bring him to his home. Sad his heart that night across the water as he went toward the ancient home, for well he knew that father, mother, sister, and brother, all had been slain upon that fearful night of battle. With sinking heart he paddled on until he saw the ruins of the Raven Village,— charred, ugly posts and beams the only signs of former greatness.

Once he was awakened by his pursuers as they paddled close along the shore

CHAPTER FIFTEEN

THE RESCUE OF NAIDA

SCARCE had his canoe touched shore before the survivors of that once great village swarmed round him. Warm his welcome and swift their questions. Then came Motana. Great his joy when told that Naida still lived, but greater when he looked upon her token message. Quickly he called his warriors about him.

"Who is brave enough to go with me to wrest my sweetheart-wife from the fearful Yaklus?"

From every man came the shout, "I will go!"

"Eight men are all I want," said Motana, "eight men who can drive a racing canoe as never a craft was driven before, eight men who know no fear of man or angry ocean. This must be a victory of cunning, speed, and courage—not of numbers. Make ready our fastest canoe of racing. Oil and polish the wood until it glistens in the sun; then it will skim the wave like a living thing. Great is my spirit power over boiling surf and raging whirlpool. Great is my knowledge of the monster that writhes in the ocean's depths and destroys the luckless ones. In the dark night we will go and take my Naida. Yaklus and his warriors will pursue us. Then we will take our way through the fearful gorge of Hyal, where the waters roar with a voice of thunder, where the spray dashes high and the evil spirits of the ocean devour all who dare their anger. My spirit strength will take us through, but Yaklus, whose power is for war, not for water monsters, will meet his death."

Shouted the men:

"You are our chief! Your thought is big! Whom will you take?"

"Those who know the water best. Those whose arms are the strongest with the paddle."

Two full nights they paddled fast. In the third, in the final hour of the darkness, they brought their canoe close to the village of Yaklus. In the late sleeping hours all was quiet. No man spoke, no dog barked. Motana stepped ashore and crept along toward the chieftain's house. Creeping, crawling, to the secret door he came. He pushed upon it. O smile of good fortune! It gave before his stealthy touch. He crawled inside. He scarcely touched the sleeping Naida before her hand reached out to tell him she had wakened. With bated breath they slipped away. Once outside, they sped like deer toward the waiting canoe. No word was spoken, no time lost, ere it shot across the water and away. In this race for life a moment wasted might be death for all.

Scarcely had they started when Yaklus woke and found his captive gone. With a bellowing roar he rushed through the great house.

"She is gone! She is gone! We must pursue her!"

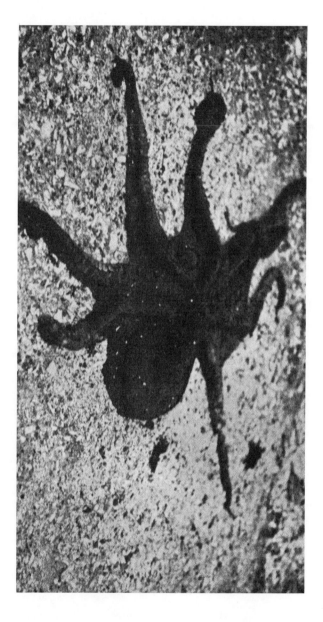

Great is my knowledge of the monster that writhes in the ocean's depths

They rushed upon the beach and saw Motana and Naida speeding far away upon the water.

"Waken! Waken! Tribesmen!"

"Waken and follow!"

"Let us crush them!"

"Let us take their heads!"

"No trick so bold as this was ever played. Well I know it was the son of Kenada! Short life to him!"

CHAPTER SIXTEEN

THE DEATH OF YAKLUS

YELLING, howling, the Yaklus horde had quickly manned three canoes, and then away. Madly they drove their craft across the water. Like a pack of baying wolves upon the scent they howled and shouted as their paddles rose and fell. Far across the water the fugitives heard that call. Well they knew the need of speed and endurance, for it was a full half day's race to the boiling gorge of Hyal. On they sped, and ever on came Yaklus and his howling pack. But little knew they of Motana's thought. Who could dream that he would attempt the boiling whirlpool gorge?

As the day drew on, the fleeing ones turned sharply to the left and shot within the walls of the dread gorge that bore the name of the Evil Ones. To lure their victim on, the waters first flow with low and subtle murmur like the whispering breeze across the forest tops, but all too soon the gorge shows its vicious, all-consuming greed and anger.

When the fleeing ones shot between the somber walls the pursuers howled with rage and disappointment. Yaklus yelled, "Where such a youth dares go we dare follow." But despite his frenzied urging the men held back.

"Those who enter here at flow or ebb of tide make widows of their wives."

Madly they drove their craft across the water

"Are you cowards? Are you women, that you hesitate to follow where an untried youth has shown the way? Have I lived to see the day when my tribesmen, my warriors, have not the courage to follow where I lead? Do you come? Or must I hurl the cry of 'Cowards' at you?"

Again they cried: "While we hang our heads and play with words we are sweeping on to death. Even now the tide's sullen roar drowns our words. The gods alone can save us. Let every man reach out in supplication."

"Ho, ho!" roared the mighty Yaklus, "if we are to die let us die as Kwakiutl should. Every man to his paddle, and now to fight these foaming rapids."

Bravely the brawny paddlers struggled with the raging, roaring tide.

The torrent lifted,—sank,—whirled into billowy crests and sucking whirlpools.

From the top of the crests the canoes plunged headlong into the frothing surge,—spun like feathers in the sucking funnels.

Men bawled themselves hoarse shouting courage to companions, but naught was heard save the roar of angry waters.

Leading well ahead were Motana and his Raven men. Their skill seemed magic as with mighty thrust of paddle they dodged and twisted through the swirling, angry waters.

Now,—they shoot along a high-piled crest of rolling breakers!

Now,—headlong into the surging billows, their canoe lost to sight!

Again upon a high-tossed crest!

And now,—courage, all!

They have reached the great fall, the most dangerous whirlpool of the gorge!

Beyond, the waters flow calm and peaceful, but few there are who have ever reached them.

The final, fearful plunge!

Motana has conquered the Evil Ones; his canoe floats on the tranquil waters.

With fear and desperation the Yaklus men fight on. Small thought have they of following Motana now. 'Tis all of self and precious life. Scarce have they reached the raging waters ere the foremost canoe plunges from crest to whirlpool, spins about and sinks from sight. Another tosses high, careens, and, bottom upward, drifts on with no hand to guide it.

Bravely the canoe of Yaklus meets and battles with the surging waters. On it plunges and pitches until that final, roaring fall. Then, like the monster of the deep, it springs its full length in the air,—and plunges head-on into the angry, all-devouring pool!

Amid the roar of water and the howl of men, unheard is the wail of the fearful Yaklus.

They shot within the walls of the dread gorge

Indian Days of the Long Ago, from which the illustration above is taken, is the first volume of the Indian Life and Indian Lore Series. It pictures a boy's life among the Salish, a western tribe of the Rocky Mountain valleys, at the time when the buffalo still roamed the plains.